LOADED WITH BENEFITS JOURNAL

Living the Believer's Life of Privilege: Ten Weeks of Personal Reflections

Daisy Buckner

LOADED WITH BENEFITS JOURNAL

Table of Contents

About This Journal.. 1

Week 1 - Living Royally - Day 1...................................... 2

Week 1 - Living Royally - Day 2...................................... 4

Week 1 - Living Royally - Day 3...................................... 6

Week 1 - Living Royally - Day 4...................................... 8

Week 1 - Living Royally - Day 5...................................... 10

Week 2 - God's Loving Care - Day 1................................ 12

Week 2 - God's Loving Care - Day 2................................ 14

Week 2 - God's Loving Care - Day 3................................ 16

Week 2 - God's Loving Care - Day 4................................ 18

Week 2 - God's Loving Care - Day 5................................ 20

Week 3 - Living the Promise - Day 1............................... 22

Week 3 - Living the Promise - Day 2............................... 24

Week 3 - Living the Promise - Day 3............................... 26

Week 3 - Living the Promise - Day 4............................... 28

Week 3 - Living the Promise - Day 5............................... 30

Week 4 - Overcoming Anxiety - Day 1............................. 32

Week 4 - Overcoming Anxiety - Day 2............................. 34

Week 4 - Overcoming Anxiety - Day 3............................. 36

Week 4 - Overcoming Anxiety - Day 4............................. 38

Week 4 - Overcoming Anxiety - Day 5............................. 40

Week 5 - Being Obedient - Day 1 42

Week 5 - Being Obedient - Day 2 44

Week 5 - Being Obedient - Day 3 46

Week 5 - Being Obedient - Day 4 48

Week 5 - Being Obedient - Day 5 50

Week 6 - Being a Conqueror - Day 1 52

Week 6 - Being a Conqueror - Day 2 54

Week 6 - Being a Conqueror - Day 3 56

Week 6 - Being a Conqueror - Day 4 58

Week 6 - Being a Conqueror - Day 5 60

Week 7 - Renewing Strength - Day 1 62

Week 7 - Renewing Strength - Day 2 64

Week 7 - Renewing Strength - Day 3 66

Week 7 - Renewing Strength - Day 4 68

Week 7 - Renewing Strength - Day 5 70

Week 8 - Communicating With Our Father - Day 1 72

Week 8 - Communicating With Our Father - Day 2 74

Week 8 - Communicating With Our Father - Day 3 76

Week 8 - Communicating With Our Father - Day 4 78

Week 8 - Communicating With Our Father - Day 5 80

Week 9 - The Greatest Gift - Day 1 82

Week 9 - The Greatest Gift - Day 2 84

Week 9 - The Greatest Gift - Day 3 86

Week 9 - The Greatest Gift - Day 4 88

Week 9 - The Greatest Gift - Day 5 90

Week 10 - Enjoying God's Favor - Day 1 92

Week 10 - Enjoying God's Favor - Day 2 94

Week 10 - Enjoying God's Favor - Day 3 96

Week 10 - Enjoying God's Favor - Day 4 98

Week 10 - Enjoying God's Favor - Day 5 100

This is a companion journal to the book *LOADED WITH BENEFITS, Living the Believer's Life of Privilege: Ten Weeks of Personal Study* that I co-authored with my husband, Ollie. It contains reflections from the book combined with inspirational Scriptures for daily meditation. In this journal you will record your personal thoughts and insights as you meditate on the Scriptures each day. It is my prayer that you will find joy, encouragement, peace and hope as you reap the "benefits" of God's favor on your life each and every day of your life. I pray that as you seek God daily, He will show you great and mighty things that you do not know *(Jeremiah 33:3)*. May God wonderfully bless you as you study and meditate on His Word.

- Daisy Buckner

Week 1 - Living Royally - Day 1

"Thus saith the LORD, thy Redeemer, the Holy One of Israel; I am the LORD thy God which teacheth thee to profit, which leadeth thee by the way that thou shouldest go" *(Isaiah 48:17)*.

✝ Thought for the Day ✝

"As God leads us in the way that we should go, it is up to us to exercise our 'free will' and follow His lead. Now that we are out of our 'wilderness experience,' we must not forget how God brought us through" *(Loaded With Benefits,* Page 5).

Your Personal Reflections

_____

_____

_____

_____

_____

_____

_____

_____

_____

Notes

"Watch ye, stand fast in the faith, quit you like men, be strong" (*I Corinthians 16:13*).

† Thought for the Day †

"Considering the enormous task before us as we live this 'life of royalty,' it is important that we stand fast in the faith knowing that we can do all things through Christ Who strengthens us" (*Loaded With Benefits*, Pages 6-7).

Your Personal Reflections

_____

_____

_____

_____

_____

_____

_____

_____

_____

_____

Notes

"The LORD is my strength and my shield; my heart trusted in Him, and I am helped: therefore my heart greatly rejoiceth; and with my song will I praise Him" *(Psalm 28:7)*.

† Thought for the Day †

"Because we know that God is good, merciful, and faithful, we can stand on His promise, in faith, to provide the substance (things seen) of our hope (things unseen). However, we must remember that, '. . . Faith, if it hath not works, is dead, being alone' *(James 2:17)*. Our faith must be active faith, doing faith, the faith that motivates us to 'Press toward the mark for the prize of the high calling of God in Christ Jesus'" *(Loaded With Benefits, Page 7)*.

Your Personal Reflections

_____

_____

_____

_____

_____

_____

_____

_____

Notes

"For the mountains shall depart, and the hills be removed; but My kindness shall not depart from thee, neither shall the covenant of My peace be removed, saith the LORD that hath mercy on thee" *(Isaiah 54:10)*.

† Thought for the Day †

"It does not matter what is going on around us, we can rest assured (in faith) that God is there for us, He will see us through, for '. . . we are His people and the sheep of His pasture'" *(Loaded With Benefit,* Page 7*)*.

Your Personal Reflections

_____

_____

_____

_____

_____

_____

_____

_____

_____

Notes

"Let your light so shine before men, that they may see your good works, and glorify your Father which is in Heaven" (*Matthew 5:16*).

† Thought for the Day †

"As a part of the privilege of being a member of the 'Royal Family' comes the responsibility of being a good representative of the family" (*Loaded With Benefits*, Page 8).

Your Personal Reflections

_____

_____

_____

_____

_____

_____

_____

_____

_____

_____

Notes

"When the poor and needy seek water, and there is none, and their tongue faileth for thirst, I the LORD will hear them, I the God of Israel will not forsake them. I will open rivers in high places, and fountains in the midst of the valleys: I will make the wilderness a pool of water, and the dry land springs of water" (*Isaiah 41:17-18*).

† Thought for the Day †

"God assures us that in our distress, He will be there for us. He will not forsake us. He will hold our hand and keep us" (*Loaded With Benefits*, Page 16).

Your Personal Reflections

_____

_____

_____

_____

_____

_____

_____

_____

_____

Notes

"When thou passest through the waters, I will be with thee; and through the rivers, they shall not overflow thee: when thou walkest through the fire, thou shalt not be burned; neither shall the flame kindle upon thee" *(Isaiah 43:2).*

† Thought for the Day †

"No matter what we are going through, God will lovingly care for us. He will make a way for us. We are never powerless in a situation, because God is our constant source of power. When we are weak in our physical body, we can always look to God for our renewed strength" *(Loaded With Benefits, Page 16).*

Your Personal Reflections

_____

_____

_____

_____

_____

_____

_____

_____

Notes

"I will go before thee, and make the crooked places straight: I will break in pieces the gates of brass, and cut in sunder the bars of iron: And I will give thee the treasures of darkness, and hidden riches of secret places, that thou mayest know that I, the LORD, which call thee by thy name, am the God of Israel" *(Isaiah 45:2-3)*.

† Thought for the Day †

"There is nothing too hard for God. He can and will supply every need as He lovingly cares for His own. We can count on this. Our faith will sustain us when all else fails" *(Loaded With Benefits*, Page 16).

Your Personal Reflections

_____

_____

_____

_____

_____

_____

_____

_____

Notes

"For I know the thoughts that I think toward you, saith the LORD, thoughts of peace, and not of evil, to give you an expected end. Then shall ye call upon Me, and ye shall go and pray unto Me, and I will hearken unto you. And ye shall seek Me, and find Me, when ye shall search for Me with all your heart" *(Jeremiah 29:11-13).*

† Thought for the Day †

"God has resolved to guide, direct, protect and provide for His people" *(Loaded With Benefits,* Page 18).

Your Personal Reflections

_____

_____

_____

_____

_____

_____

_____

_____

_____

_____

Notes

"Come now, and let us reason together, saith the LORD: though your sins be as scarlet, they shall be as white as snow; though they be red like crimson, they shall be as wool" (*Isaiah 1:18*).

† Thought for the Day †

"In God, we find forgiveness through His Son. Once we come to God and are made worthy through the Blood of the Lamb, it is very important from that point on, that we strive to be obedient to our Father, in order to reap the full benefit of our inheritance as children of The King" (*Loaded With Benefits*, Pages 18-19).

Your Personal Reflections

_____

_____

_____

_____

_____

_____

_____

_____

_____

_____

Notes

"Cast thy burden upon the LORD, and He shall sustain thee: He shall never suffer the righteous to be moved" *(Psalm 55:22).*

✝ Thought for the Day ✝

"Whatever our circumstance, we can rejoice knowing that God is the One that is in control" *(Loaded With Benefits,* Page 24).

Your Personal Reflections

_____

_____

_____

_____

_____

_____

_____

_____

_____

_____

_____

_____

Notes

"For His anger endureth but a moment; in His favour is life: weeping may endure for a night, but joy cometh in the morning" *(Psalm 30:5).*

† Thought for the Day †

"We do not have to wait for the battle to be over to shout. We can shout now, because we have the victory through Christ Jesus. When we feel, faint, when we become weary, we are to go to the source of our supply, our God" *(Loaded With Benefits, Page 24).*

Your Personal Reflections

_____

_____

_____

_____

_____

_____

_____

_____

_____

_____

Notes

"O taste and see that the LORD is good: blessed is the man that trusteth in Him. O fear the LORD, ye His saints: for there is no want to them that fear Him. The young lions do lack, and suffer hunger: but they that seek the LORD shall not want any good thing" *(Psalm 34:8-10)*.

† Thought for the Day †

"We serve a loving God Who cares about every step that we take in this journey here on earth. We serve a wise God Who knows all about us. We serve a powerful God, Who is able to do all. There is nothing too hard for Him. We serve an ever-present God Who will not leave us or forsake us. We serve a faithful God Who is ever present and will keep His promise to us. He is indeed our All-in-All" *(Loaded With Benefits, Page 25)*.

Your Personal Reflections

_____

_____

_____

_____

_____

_____

_____

Notes

"But the LORD is with me as a mighty terrible One: therefore my persecutors shall stumble, and they shall not prevail: they shall be greatly ashamed; for they shall not prosper: their everlasting confusion shall never be forgotten" (*Jeremiah 20:11*).

† Thought for the Day †

"From the Scriptures, it is evident that those who fight against God's people do so in vain. They have lost even before the battle begins" (*Loaded With Benefits*, Page 27).

Your Personal Reflections

_____

_____

_____

_____

_____

_____

_____

_____

_____

Notes

"Or what man is there of you, whom if his son ask bread, will he give him a stone? Or if he ask a fish, will he give him a serpent? If ye then, being evil, know how to give good gifts unto your children, how much more shall your Father which is in Heaven give good things to them that ask Him?" *(Matthew 7:9-11)*

† Thought for the Day †

"We know that we tend to take great care of those who are valuable to us. Then think of how much more care God is able to give to those who are valuable to Him" *(Loaded With Benefits, Page 28)*.

Your Personal Reflections

_____

_____

_____

_____

_____

_____

_____

_____

_____

Notes

"Be careful for nothing; but in every thing by prayer and supplication with thanksgiving let your requests be made known unto God. And the peace of God, which passeth all understanding, shall keep your hearts and minds through Christ Jesus" (*Philippians 4:6-7*).

† Thought for the Day †

"Whatever the situation or circumstance, we are to take it to God, and rest in Him as He works things out for us" (*Loaded With Benefits, page 33*).

Your Personal Reflections

_____

_____

_____

_____

_____

_____

_____

_____

_____

Notes

"Cast thy burden upon the LORD, and He shall sustain thee: He shall never suffer the righteous to be moved" (*Psalm 55:22*).

✝ Thought for the Day ✝

"In obedience to God, when the load is too heavy for us, we are to let Him have our burdens. He can bear them so much better than we can." (*Loaded With Benefits*, Page 34).

Your Personal Reflections

_____

_____

_____

_____

_____

_____

_____

_____

_____

_____

_____

Notes

"Trust in the LORD with all thine heart; and lean not unto thine own understanding. In all thy ways acknowledge Him, and He shall direct thy paths" *(Proverbs 3:5-6)*.

† Thought for the Day †

"We may be in a situation and feel that we are stuck and there is no way out. However, for us, as children of God, Jesus is The Way. He suffered, bled and died just for us" *(Loaded With Benefits, Page 34)*.

Your Personal Reflections

_____

_____

_____

_____

_____

_____

_____

_____

_____

_____

Notes

"He will not suffer thy foot to be moved: He that keepeth thee will not slumber" (*Psalm 121:3*).

✝ Thought for the Day ✝

"Many times, we may be so busy looking at our situation, analyzing it, worrying and wondering what we must do, and we fail to see what God is already doing for us in the situation. God does not sleep on the job. He is always busy working for us, in us and through us, even in what we might think is the worst of circumstances" (*Loaded With Benefits*, Page 34).

Your Personal Reflections

_____

_____

_____

_____

_____

_____

_____

_____

_____

Notes

"Many are the afflictions of the righteous: but the LORD delivereth him out of them all" (*Psalm 34:19*).

† Thought for the Day †

"Although trouble will come, in the midst of the trials, God is
there and He will deliver His own" (*Loaded With Benefits*, Page 35).

Your Personal Reflections

_____

_____

_____

_____

_____

_____

_____

_____

_____

_____

_____

_____

Notes

"Let every soul be subject unto the higher powers. For there is no power but of God: the powers that be are ordained of God. Whosoever therefore resisteth the power, resisteth the ordinance of God: and they that resist shall receive to themselves damnation" (*Romans 13:1-2*).

† Thought for the Day †

"Principally, we must be obedient to God. Being obedient to God is simply doing what He has commanded us to do. Christ obeyed the Father, giving us the supreme example of obedience" (*Loaded With Benefits*, Page 42).

Your Personal Reflections

_____

_____

_____

_____

_____

_____

_____

_____

_____

Notes

". . . The LORD God, merciful and gracious, longsuffering, and abundant in goodness and truth, keeping mercy for thousands, forgiving iniquity and transgression and sin, and that will by no means clear the guilty; visiting the iniquity of the fathers upon the children, and upon the children's children, unto the third and to the fourth generation" (*Exodus 34:6-7*).

† Thought for the Day †

"We might think that something or someone is the best thing since sliced bread, but if God tells us that it is not good for us, then it is not good for us. If we disobey God, then there are consequences for us" (*Loaded With Benefits*, Page 44).

Your Personal Reflections

_____

_____

_____

_____

_____

_____

_____

_____

Notes

"He that hath My commandments, and keepeth them, he it is that loveth Me: and he that loveth Me shall be loved of My Father, and I will love him, and will manifest Myself to him" (*John 14:21*).

† Thought for the Day †

"We can rejoice in the love of God at all times, knowing that His love never fails" (*Loaded With Benefits*, Page 44).

Your Personal Reflections

_____

_____

_____

_____

_____

_____

_____

_____

_____

_____

Notes

"In His presence is fullness of joy; at His right hand there are pleasures for evermore" (*Psalm 16:11*).

† Thought for the Day †

"It is important to note that when we are obedient in praising our God and rejoicing in Him, we are blessed by that very act" (*Loaded With Benefits*, Page 45).

Your Personal Reflections

_____

_____

_____

_____

_____

_____

_____

_____

_____

_____

_____

Notes

"The righteous cry, and the LORD heareth, and delivereth them out of all their troubles" (*Psalm 34:17*).

† Thought for the Day †

"No matter what circumstance we are in, whether in times of sadness or despair, we can rest assured that God is with us" (*Loaded With Benefits*, Page 45).

Your Personal Reflections

_____

_____

_____

_____

_____

_____

_____

_____

_____

_____

Notes

Notes

Week 6 - Being a Conqueror - Day 1

"No weapon that is formed against thee shall prosper; and every tongue that shall rise against thee in judgment thou shalt condemn. This is the heritage of the servants of the LORD, and their righteousness is of Me, saith the LORD" (*Isaiah 54:17*).

† Thought for the Day †

'As servants of God, we are often under attack by 'the enemy' but we must remember that because we belong to God, we have a ready defense that is our heritage" (*Loaded With Benefits*, Page 51).

Your Personal Reflections

Notes

"The LORD shall cause thine enemies that rise up against thee to be smitten before thy face: they shall come out against thee one way, and flee before thee seven ways" (*Deuteronomy 28:7*).

† Thought for the Day †

"When doubts, fears and uncertainties arise, we can rejoice in the hope that is in our all powerful, all wise, and loving Father, knowing that He will be faithful to us. The question for us is: Can we be faithful to Him?" (*Loaded With Benefits*, Page 53).

Your Personal Reflections

_____

_____

_____

_____

_____

_____

_____

_____

_____

_____

_____

_____

Notes

"Be not afraid of sudden fear, neither of the desolation of the wicked, when it cometh. For the LORD shall be thy confidence, and shall keep thy foot from being taken" (*Proverbs 3:25-26*).

† Thought for the Day †

"We must listen to God and do the things that He instructs us to do. We know that we can depend on the fulfillment of His promises" (*Loaded With Benefits*, Page 53).

Your Personal Reflections

Notes

'Behold, all they that were incensed against thee shall be ashamed and confounded: they shall be as nothing; and they that strive with thee shall perish. Thou shalt seek them, and shalt not find them, even them that contended with thee: they that war against thee shall be as nothing, and as a thing of nought" (*Isaiah 41:11-12*).

† Thought for the Day †

"We have the assurance that we need not be fearful, that we can trust that God is with us and will uphold us" (*Loaded With Benefits*, Page 52).

Your Personal Reflections

Notes

Week 6 - Being a Conqueror - Day 5

"The rod of the wicked shall not rest upon the lot of the righteous" (*Psalm 125:3*).

† Thought for the Day †

"Throughout God's Word we find the assurance that He is our Deliverer, that He shall deliver us from the wicked and save us, because we trust Him" (*Loaded With Benefits*, Page 52).

Your Personal Reflections

_____

_____

_____

_____

_____

_____

_____

_____

_____

_____

_____

_____

Notes

"He giveth power to the faint; and to them that have no might He increaseth strength. Even the youths shall faint and be weary, and the young men shall utterly fall: But they that wait upon the LORD shall renew their strength; they shall mount up with wings as eagles; they shall run, and not be weary; and they shall walk, and not faint" (*Isaiah 40:29-31*).

† Thought for the Day †

"Both young and old, will at times become weary; but, God has promised to renew our strength so that we will once again soar as eagles" (*Loaded With Benefits*, Page 57).

Your Personal Reflections

_____

_____

_____

_____

_____

_____

_____

_____

_____

Notes

"Though I walk in the midst of trouble, Thou wilt revive me: Thou shalt stretch forth Thine hand against the wrath of mine enemies, and Thy right hand shall save me" (*Psalm 138:7*).

† Thought for the Day †

There are times when we, as workers for Christ, feel so tired that we do not think that we can keep going. Yet, we know that there is a lot that we must do. At times like this, we must remember that our 'Employer' is the source of our strength" (*Loaded With Benefits*, Page 57).

Your Personal Reflections

_____

_____

_____

_____

_____

_____

_____

_____

_____

_____

Notes

"For unto whomsoever much is given, of him shall be much required: and to whom men have committed much, of him they will ask the more" (*Luke 12:48*).

† Thought for the Day †

"God requires that we make use of all that He has given us. He has given us gifts for His glory" (*Loaded With Benefits*, Page 59).

Your Personal Reflections

_____

_____

_____

_____

_____

_____

_____

_____

_____

_____

_____

_____

_____

_____

Notes

"...What doth the LORD thy God require of thee, but to fear the LORD thy God, to walk in all His ways, and to love Him, and to serve the LORD thy God with all thy heart and with all thy soul" *Deuteronomy 10:12*).

† Thought for the Day †

"Realizing that we are to faithfully serve God, we must allow Him to position us so that He can use us effectively. We are His tools, and as with all tools, we occasionally need to be sharpened in order to do the best possible job for God as He works in us 'both to will and to do His good pleasure'" (*Loaded With Benefits*, Page 60).

Your Personal Reflections

_____

_____

_____

_____

_____

_____

_____

_____

Notes

"But whoso looketh into the perfect law of liberty, and continueth therein, he being not a forgetful hearer, but a doer of the work, this man shall be blessed in his deed" *(James 1:25).*

† Thought for the Day †

"We must be careful that our steps are ordered in God's Word *(Psalm 119:133),* for it is through this that we are blessed" (*Loaded With Benefits,* Page 61).

Your Personal Reflections

_____

_____

_____

_____

_____

_____

_____

_____

_____

_____

Notes

Write a prayer thanking
God

"Give unto the LORD the glory due unto His name; worship the LORD in the beauty of holiness" (*Psalm 29:2*).

† Thought for the Day †

"Our communication with our Father should not be simply relegating our prayer life to asking God to supply our needs. If this is what we are doing, then we are missing some key ingredients in our prayer life that could make us more effective as prayer warriors" (*Loaded With Benefits*, Page 65).

Your Personal Reflections

_____

_____

_____

_____

_____

_____

_____

_____

_____

_____

Notes

"Rejoice in the LORD, ye righteous; and give thanks at the re-
membrance of His holiness" (*Psalm 97:12*).

✝ Thought for the Day ✝

"Many times our prayers are nothing more than a shopping list.
We ask God to supply our needs without actually giving Him the
adoration or thanksgiving that is due Him" (*Loaded With Benefits*, Page
66).

Your Personal Reflections

_____

_____

_____

_____

_____

_____

_____

_____

_____

_____

_____

_____

Notes

"Be careful for nothing; but in every thing by prayer and supplication with thanksgiving let your requests be made known unto God. And the peace of God, which passeth all understanding, shall keep your hearts and minds through Christ Jesus" (*Philippians 4:6-7*).

† Thought for the Day †

"It is important that we take the time to 'be with God' as we pray, to get personal and talk with Him as the friend that He really is. We should make our prayer time more than just a time to go shopping for what we want from God, as we on occasions, run through a thanks to Him" (*Loaded With Benefits*, Page 66).

Your Personal Reflections

_____

_____

_____

_____

_____

_____

_____

_____

_____

Notes

"Confess your faults one to another, and pray one for another, that ye may be healed. The effectual fervent prayer of a righteous man availeth much" (*James 5:16*).

† Thought for the Day †

"Realizing that as believers in Christ we are co-laborers for the Kingdom, we must pray for one another. We are not to be selfish as we enjoy the rich heritage that we have been given. At times, we may see others who are overwhelmed and we feel helpless. The one thing that we all can do in any situation is pray" (*Loaded With Benefits*, Page 67).

Your Personal Reflections

_____

_____

_____

_____

_____

_____

_____

_____

_____

_____

Notes

And shall not God avenge His own elect, which cry day and night unto Him, though He bear long with them? I tell you that He will avenge them speedily" (*Luke 18:7-8*).

† Thought for the Day †

"We need not let anxiety and worry stop us from enjoying our rich heritage. We need only to call [on] God" (*Loaded With Benefits, Page 68*).

Your Personal Reflections

_____

_____

_____

_____

_____

_____

_____

_____

_____

_____

Notes

"For ye have not received the spirit of bondage again to fear; but ye have received the Spirit of adoption, whereby we cry, Abba, Father. The Spirit itself beareth witness with our spirit, that we are the children of God: And if children, then heirs; heirs of God, and joint-heirs with Christ" (*Romans 8:15-17*).

† Thought for the Day †

"As children of God, not only are we blessed with salvation in the next life, we are also blessed in this life, for our Father is all-wise, all-knowing, all-powerful; and, He is very concerned about the quality of life of His children (*Loaded With Benefits*, Page 73).

Your Personal Reflections

_____

_____

_____

_____

_____

_____

_____

_____

_____

_____

Notes

Therefore I say unto you, What things soever ye desire, when ye pray, believe that ye receive them, and ye shall have them" (*Mark 11:24*).

† Thought for the Day †

"There is one very important thing that is required of us as we ask according to His will. And that is, we must have faith to believe" (*Loaded With Benefits*, Page 74).

Your Personal Reflections

_____

_____

_____

_____

_____

_____

_____

_____

_____

_____

_____

_____

Notes

"And this is the confidence that we have in Him, that, if we ask any thing according to His will, He heareth us: And if we know that He hear us, whatsoever we ask, we know that we have the petitions that we desired of Him" (*1 John 5:14-15*).

† Thought for the Day †

"Salvation in the next life is the *Greatest Gift of All*. With this gift comes the fringe benefit of being able to go to God in faith, and find help in any situation in this life, all because of the grace of God" (*Loaded With Benefits, Page 74*).

Your Personal Reflections

_____

_____

_____

_____

_____

_____

_____

_____

_____

_____

_____

Notes

...I have spoken it, I will also bring it to pass; I have purposed it, will also do it" (*Isaiah 46:11*).

† Thought for the Day †

"Embedded throughout God's Word, we find the assurance that our Heavenly Father will keep His promises to His children. He is the 'God of truth'" (*Loaded With Benefits*, Page 77).

Your Personal Reflections

_____

_____

_____

_____

_____

_____

_____

_____

_____

_____

_____

Notes

"God is not a man, that He should lie; neither the Son of Man, that He should repent: hath He said, and shall He not do it? or hath He spoken, and shall He not make it good?" (*Numbers 23:19*)

† Thought for the Day †

"God assures us that He will deliver. We need only to try Him, to test Him now and see that He will" (*Loaded With Benefits*, Page 77).

Your Personal Reflections

_____

_____

_____

_____

_____

_____

_____

_____

_____

_____

_____

Notes

"My son, forget not my law; but let thine heart keep my commandments: For length of days, and long life, and peace, shall they add to thee. Let not mercy and truth forsake thee: bind them about thy neck; write them upon the table of thine heart: So shalt thou find favour and good understanding in the sight of God and man" (*Proverbs 3:1-4*).

✝ Thought for the Day ✝

"By definition, to be favored by someone, is to have his or her kindness and good will. To be favored by God, is to be abundantly blessed with His loving kindness" (*Loaded With Benefits*, Page 83).

Your Personal Reflections

_____

_____

_____

_____

_____

_____

_____

_____

Notes

"When a man's ways please the LORD, he maketh even his enemies to be at peace with him" *(Proverbs 16:7)*.

† Thought for the Day †

"As God's children, in keeping His commandments not only will we have the favor of God, but God will cause man to favor us as well" *(Loaded With Benefits, Page 83)*.

Your Personal Reflections

Notes

The righteous cry, and the LORD heareth, and delivereth them out of all their troubles. The LORD is nigh unto them that are of a broken heart; and saveth such as be of a contrite spirit. Many are the afflictions of the righteous: but the LORD delivereth him out of them all" (*Psalm 34:17-19*).

† Thought for the Day †

"The fact that we are favored by God, does not mean that we will not have troubles. However, it does mean that with His favor, we can be delivered out of any trouble" (*Loaded With Benefits*, Page 84).

Your Personal Reflections

_____

_____

_____

_____

_____

_____

_____

_____

_____

_____

Notes

"O fear the LORD, ye His saints: for there is no want to them that fear Him. The young lions do lack, and suffer hunger: but they that seek the LORD shall not want any good thing" (*Psalm 34:9-10*).

† Thought for the Day †

"'True riches' are in our God Who is eternal. In Him we have treasures that are lasting and immeasurable" (*Loaded With Benefits*, Page 86).

Your Personal Reflections

_____

_____

_____

_____

_____

_____

_____

_____

_____

_____

_____

_____

Notes

Now therefore hearken unto Me, O ye children: for blessed are they that keep My ways. Hear instruction, and be wise, and refuse not. Blessed is the man that heareth Me, watching daily at My gates, waiting at the posts of My doors. For whoso findeth Me findeth life, and shall obtain favour of the LORD" (*Proverbs 8:32-35*).

† Thought for the Day †

"Yes, we who are children of the most High God, will daily receive the benefits of His favor. The Lord, our God, has spoken, 'Blessed be the Lord, Who daily loadeth us with benefits, even the God of our salvation' (*Psalm 68:19*). To Him be glory, power, majesty, and dominion, both now and forever. Amen" (*Loaded With Benefits*, Page 87).

Your Personal Reflections

_____

_____

_____

_____

_____

_____

_____

_____

_____

Notes

About the Author

Daisy Buckner is a lifelong educator who resides in Marietta, Georgia with her husband, Ollie. She is currently a professor at Life University in Marietta. Daisy previously co-authored the companion book for this journal with her husband. The companion book, *LOADED WITH BENEFITS, Living the Believer's Life & Privilege: Ten Weeks of Personal Study* (ISBN 978-0-557-04460-3) is available online at...

http://stores.lulu.com/bucknerschristianbooks and also on Amazon.com